D0254814

TEILHARD DE CHARDIN

MAKERS OF CONTEMPORARY THEOLOGY

EDITORS:

The Rev. Professor D. E. NINEHAM
The Rev. E. H. ROBERTSON

TEILHARD DE CHARDIN

by

BERNARD TOWERS

JOHN KNOX PRESS
ATLANTA

Published in Great Britain by
The Carey Kingsgate Press Limited, London, England, 1966
and in the United States by
John Knox Press, 1966

Sixth printing 1975

Standard Book Number: 8042-0723-2
Library of Congress Catalog Card Number: 66-15515
© Bernard Towers
First published in 1966
Printed in the United States

Contents

Introduction

PIERRE TEILHARD DE CHARDIN, of the Society of Jesus, died on 10 April, 1955, at the age of seventy-three. It was Easter Sunday. He had once said that of all the days of the year he would most like to die on the day of the resurrection. He could have had little inkling, though, that it would be on that particular Easter Day that he was to undergo his 'change of state' (which was how he always looked on death) and join the risen Christ. He was living at the time in the Jesuit house in New York, continuing his scientific studies and his writing at the Wenner-Gren Foundation. On the morning of 10 April, after saying his own mass, he attended the high mass in the cathedral. After lunch he went to a concert, walking through the park in the spring sunshine, and had gone on for tea with friends. There, without any warning, he had a heart attack, and fell on the floor. He regained consciousness for only a few moments before he died. He is buried in the Jesuit cemetery just outside New York.

At the time of his death his name was known to quite a large circle of personal friends in Europe, Asia, Africa and America – he never visited Australia, but in the other four continents he travelled widely, and everywhere he went his capacity for friendship, his integrity and goodwill, won for him the affection and loyalty of people of all faiths and none. His name was known, too, and highly respected, in the scientific world of geology and palaeontology, where he had earned a world-wide reputation. By his superiors and fellow-members of the Jesuit Order, and in other ecclesiastical circles including Rome, he was known as a man of great spiritual insight, and a dedicated searcher after truth. But his thought was too daring, and was usually considered too dangerous (except in the case of scientific articles, of which he published more than 150) to be approved for publication by those to whom, in accordance with his vow of obedience, he was required to submit his articles and books. The result was

that at the time of his death his epoch-making ideas were unknown except to a very small number of people, comparatively
speaking. 'Will anyone ever listen to me?'[1] he once wrote to his
cousin Marguerite Teillard-Chambon, in 1919, after outlining
some of the ideas that he hoped one day to see in print.

The decade since his death has seen his rhetorical question
answered a thousand times in the affirmative. With his dry
humour Teilhard might even have remarked that he would have
been more than satisfied with one hundredth part of the glaring
publicity to which he has been subjected. He was not impatient,
as some of his posthumous devotees have shown themselves to
be. His thought was too deeply rooted in his knowledge of the
natural science of development, of the long periods of time involved in the evolutionary process, for him ever to think that a
single man's vision would sweep successfully across the world at
breakneck speed. But the last few years have seen literally
thousands of articles, *mémoires*, broadcasts and book reviews,
burgeoning forth in every part of the world in increasing numbers. Many of the things that have so far been said about Teilhard
and his thought have been couched in heady, emotional terms.
This is particularly true of some enthusiasts who have 'gone
overboard' for a system of thought and action that embraces the
All in one magnificent sweep of knowledge and adoration of
alpha and omega. But it is also true of some of those, relatively
few, hostile critics, who have let emotion run away with them in
denouncing what they interpret as theological betrayal, or
scientific nonsense, or philosophical *naïveté*, or downright rub-
bish. There is something about Teilhard's euphoria, both of
thought and style, that encourages readers to let themselves be
carried away and lose their heads in a wave of passion. Any im-
balance that results is bound to produce, in time, a reaction.
There have been those who, after feeling the first flush of enthusiasm, have subsequently wondered, disappointed, how it was
that they ever allowed themselves to be 'taken in'. Actively hostile critics are then quick to seize the chance, and belabour the

[1] *The Making of a Mind* (Collins), p. 271.

former idol in a way that incenses those devotees for whom the light has far from failed.

That all this, and much more, should have happened in so short a time, is remarkable enough. It makes one think, when at times one is tempted to criticise those ecclesiastical censors who refused Teilhard permission to publish, that if he himself had been whirled into the turmoil of controversy, criticism and adulation his posthumous works have inspired, his development and output might have been severely hampered and limited. It has been argued that one effect of censorship was to prevent his correcting and modifying his ideas through discussion with colleagues. It should be remembered that within his own 'family' of the Society to which he belonged, and with friends and colleagues elsewhere, he had ample opportunity for the kind of discussion which alone is fruitful, namely critical but kindly analysis of both the roots and the flower of intellectual argument. The best commentaries on Teilhard to date are by friends who knew him well, and who discussed with him continually, both face to face and by letter. The notion that he was intellectually ostracised and isolated is a travesty.

The discipline imposed on him by the Jesuit Order in respect of publication was strict indeed. But it was nothing compared to the discipline imposed on every Christian who desires conscientiously to follow Christ. If Teilhard never experienced any real doubts or waverings about his religion he certainly never had any about his vocation as a Jesuit priest. When friends urged him to seek publication of his works by becoming a secular priest or by independent action his reply was always the same, that he was a son of St. Ignatius, and could no more think of repudiating his father in God than of repudiating his own father whose memory he revered. One can imagine Teilhard himself watching, with a wry smile, the emotional antics indulged in since his death by his fellow-men for whom he wrote the essays that have caused the controversies, for whom he suffered a good many personal misfortunes, and by whom he dearly wanted to be heard. When emotion gets out of hand, whether in positive or negative fashion, the situation calls first for control and discipline. These virtues Teilhard himself did not lack. In the face of many misunderstandings and much opposition, he says[2] 'one might well become impatient or lose heart . . . if the whole of history were not there to pledge to us that a truth once seen, even by a single mind, always ends up by imposing itself on the totality of human consciousness'. It may take time, perhaps a very long time, but some of the truths that Teilhard saw, precisely because they are based on a scientific method within which alone the quotation is valid, are of the kind that *will* eventually impose themselves on the totality of human consciousness. Teilhard's writing is full of faith in the future, of faith in God under the two aspects in which he always saw him: God *en avant* and God *en haut*, the first representing the spirit of Earth, the second that of Heaven. Teilhard reconciles, or rather refuses ever to split, these two aspects of human progress and God's purpose. Theological disquiet was inevitable. To see the theological orthodoxy of what looks like an attempt to accommodate 'the world, the flesh, and the devil', it is necessary to go back to St. Paul's vision of the pleroma, when 'nature in its turn will be set free from the tyranny of corruption, to share in the freedom of God's sons'.

Teilhard de Chardin does not sit easily in a series of booklets entitled 'Makers of Contemporary Theology'. Most of his pioneering work has only very recently become available for scholars to study and work on, and some is still unpublished. It will take time before his majestic syntheses become incorporated into a contemporary theological movement. In some ways it might have been better for this booklet to have been written half a century hence.

It is particularly odd to think of Teilhard as a 'maker of contemporary theology' if by the term one means what goes by the title 'new theology', that is the theology based on an existentialist system that stems from Kierkegaard. A great deal of Christian existentialism, with its emphasis on the personal encounter with God and his creatures, and its requirement of personal commit-

[2] *The Phenomenon of Man* (Collins), p. 218.

ment, would be completely congenial to Teilhard. No one was more committed than he, and no one faced up to personal encounters with greater faith, or hope, or love. But the streak of pessimism which runs through most of the thinking classed as 'existentialist' was wholly alien to Teilhard's thought. In a later chapter this distinction will be elaborated, and its reasons sought. Suffice it now to point out that Teilhard is no 'maker of contemporary theology' in the sense referred to. But when 'the new theology' has passed out of fashion, and become old in its turn, Teilhard's thought will remain fresh and vital. He is *sui generis*, and his insights will set a pattern which will last, because of their generality and range of application, for all time. It would be better, perhaps, to write of him under the title 'maker of the theology of the future'.

I

Life[3]

Early Influences

MARIE-JOSEPH-PIERRE TEILHARD DE CHARDIN was born on 1 May, 1881 in the family's house called Sarcenat in the Auvergne district of central France, a few miles from Clermont. The short form of his name is Pierre Teilhard (pronounced Tay-yar), the ending 'de Chardin' coming from his maternal grandmother. Other branches of the family had other suffixes added to the surname Teilhard (or Teillard as it was sometimes spelt). He was the fourth of eleven children of the marriage in 1875 of Emmanuel Teilhard with Berthe-Adèle de Dompierre d'Hornoy, who was a collateral descendant of Voltaire. When Pierre was nineteen, in the year 1900, ten of the children were alive. What with them and his cousins, with whom part of the year was always spent, his childhood must have given him ample opportunity for the development of the habit of those personal relations and friendships which were to mean so much to him in life, and which were to contribute so markedly to the development of his thought. His relations with his parents were of the warmest kind, as the published *Lettres d'Egypte 1905–1908* amply testify. Learning of his mother's death, when he was in his fifties and at the height of his power and energies in China, he said, 'To this dear and sainted mother I owe the best part of my soul.'

The expression he used here so naturally may allow a first excursion into his developed thought. It is not possible to separate him out into his 'Life' on the one hand and his 'Thought' on the other. He was all of a piece, a garment without seams, just

[3] In this chapter I have drawn heavily, for factual detail, on the masterly study of Claude Cuénot, *Teilhard de Chardin, A Biographical Study* (Burns and Oates). But for interpretations and assessments I must assume full responsibility.

as he conceived the created universe to be. When Teilhard says he owes 'the best part of his soul' to the influence of his mother he is not simply using a figure of speech. He is writing in instinctive and sustained opposition to that dualistic form of Christian thinking that regards the 'soul' as a separate substance, separately created, and infused into a body which acts as its temporary prison-house and from which it escapes, at death, to its great relief and satisfaction. For Teilhard soul and body are, during terrestrial existence, but two aspects, two faces, of the same created *person*. It is impossible to affect the one without affecting the other. The ground of our being is physical and biological. If Christ came into the world in order to save it (including men) then matter is as much an expression of God's creative activity and redemptive field as is spirit. The only question is, how can they act as the unity they ought to be? The answer is, for Teilhard, through love. When a mother cares for the physical needs of her child she is helping him to develop his soul, just as well as when she is caring for his spiritual needs. Through a multitude of loving acts from his 'dear and sainted mother' Teilhard developed a heart and soul, and a capacity for love, large enough to embrace the world.

His father was a country gentleman of means, who occupied himself with his estates and with outdoor pursuits. But he was also a scholar of merit who did good work in the field of local history. He himself used to supervise the Latin lessons of the children, and it was he who inculcated into Pierre his abiding passion for the things of nature, for stones and rocks, animals and plants, clouds and stars. The ancient volcanic district of Auvergne was full of historical and current interest for anyone with eyes to see and an inquiring mind. Teilhard later wrote of it with affection,

Auvergne moulded me . . . Auvergne served me both as museum of natural history and as wild-life preserve. Sarcenat in Auvergne gave me my first taste of the joys of discovery . . . to Auvergne I owe my delight in nature. Auvergne it was that gave me my most precious possessions: a collection of pebbles and rocks still to be found there, where I lived.[4]

The extinct volcanoes, under whose shadow he grew up, 'old as the hills', impressed the boy with their majesty and durability. And yet they had once been boiling and bubbling with suppressed energy. They themselves were not, therefore, as permanent and immutable as they seemed. But what of individual stones and pieces of metal? Teilhard at five and six years of age had a passion for these, especially for iron, his 'genie' as he called it. He has recorded what a bitter blow it was to him when he discovered, as he quickly did, that the piece of iron he treasured as incorruptible and everlasting, had in fact turned rusty. Earlier than this he had observed, again to his grief, that he himself was made of corruptible material: this was when he held out to the fire one of his curls, which had just been snipped off. When it burned up he saw with anguish that part of himself had apparently completely disappeared.

Insights acquired in childhood have a permanent effect on the personality. It would have been understandable if Pierre had turned in revulsion, as others have done, from the world of perishable nature, and sought happiness in spiritual pursuits instead, with their promise of real permanence. Had he done so the psycho-analytically inclined would have found a ready-made interpretation in terms of parental influences, especially that of his 'sainted' mother. But his mother was no gnostic or deist. She taught him Christ the Son of Man and Son of God, Christ the redeemer, Christ crucified. The incarnation really meant what it said. God came into the world, took on the corruptible attributes of the world, and redeemed it utterly. If the boy's locks appeared to be perishable, what of the sacred heart, also made of living matter?

There seems to have been no psychological struggle in the child's mind between the influence of his father and that of his mother. The balance and wholeness that he achieved in his own

[4] Cuénot, *op. cit.*, p. 3.

life, and in his 'philosophy of wholeness', suggests, what he himself has indicated, that the roots of his thinking go right down
into the soil of his childhood in the Auvergne, where they were
marvellously watered and nourished. It is interesting to note that
the same region produced another great thinker, Blaise Pascal,
with whom Teilhard has been compared.[5] But Pascal lived in a
static universe, and the 'silence of those infinite spaces' terrified
him. Teilhard's vision is fully of the twentieth century (or perhaps the twenty-first). He integrates modern scientific knowledge, of a universe in evolution, with spiritual insights into the
nature of God's activity as deep as any mystic has ever achieved.
In his system the terror of Pascal gives way to awe, wonder and
love. The physical universe itself, proceeding from God, becomes
an object of adoration, because it is an object of research. Research is adoration, says Teilhard, and gives at once a new direction and a new meaning to the time-honoured phrase *laborare est
orare*.

When he reached eleven years of age he left the shelter of the
family school-room and, following family tradition, started his
formal education at the Jesuit college at Villefranche-sur-Saône
in the Rhône. Highly intelligent and hard-working, he won many
prizes on his way through the school. The one subject in which
he did poorly was religious instruction. Not that the subject-
matter failed to interest him, but the God of the manuals was
already, perhaps, too small and mean to satisfy him. Pietistic
attitudes never impressed him (which is why he would be the
first to smile at the excessive piety with which his name has been
invoked in some quarters since his death). Pious stories of plaster-
saints and their sugary devotions bored him to tears. 'Who
would wish to spend eternity in such boring company?' he once
said, in appealing for a 'new theology' of a kind that could con-
ceivably make sense for twentieth-century man.

The task of theology is twofold, first to preserve its essential
message in all its awful grandeur, and secondly, so to express it
that it is seen to be both relevant and meaningful to each succeed-

[5] Etienne Borne, *De Pascal à Teilhard de Chardin* (Editions de Bussac, 1962).

ing age. Augustine, and later Aquinas used the knowledge and language of their day, and each set in motion a stream which pursued its course (with some setbacks, reformations and readjustments) over many centuries. Teilhard's name will be counted among such great thinkers, but with this difference. Teilhard's system is wholly dynamic, springing as it does from his certain knowledge of the evolutionary process. It is in no sense, therefore, a monolithic and static structure in the way that Thomism was in some respects. His system is an open one that represents a challenge to think and grow, rather than a comfortable support behind which the timid can shelter and weave their own new orthodoxy out of Teilhardian maxims. The method of the natural sciences was fundamental to Teilhard, the method of appealing to facts, to the phenomena, for verification of a concept.

Just as science is always open to advance and progress by virtue of a built-in mechanism of verification, so too is Teilhard's system. If science has its backwaters of stagnant ideas, where orthodoxy is ready to ignore or deny real advance, so it will probably be in the world of Teilhardiana. It is more important that the spirit of his thinking be preserved inviolate, than that his personal conclusions be accepted and committed to memory. Toward the end of *The Phenomenon of Man* he says, 'I may have gone astray at many points. It is up to others to try to do better.' This is the only proper attitude for anyone with the scholar's passion for truth. He has much to teach us, but disciples must not become slaves.

Jesuit Studies

At the age of seventeen, Teilhard decided to enter a life of religion, and chose the Jesuits because, as he put it later, he desired the 'most perfect' as examples. He was the only one of eight brothers who became a priest: the others became engineers, businessmen or Service officers. He entered the Jesuit novitiate at Aix-en-Provence in 1890 to start the long course of study and training in secular and sacred subjects, and in practical asceticism, that marks the Order. Within two years, with anticlericalism at its height in

B

France, the seminary was forced to evacuate, and came to Jersey. This marked the beginning of a lifelong contact with and affection for England.

It also marked the beginning of a serious, professional interest in geology: Jersey is singularly rich in ancient fossil-bearing rocks, and Teilhard developed an absorbing passion for their study. His spiritual development, in the cloistered calm of the seminary, was absorbing too, and for perhaps the only time in his life he was seriously tempted to give up the sciences in preference for the cloister. He later wrote, 'At that moment I would have gone off the rails if it had not been for the solid common sense of Père T. (Fr. Paul Troussard, the Novice Master). What he did, in fact, was simply to assure me that my crucified God looked for a "natural" development of my being, as well as for its sanctification.'[6]

Formal studies, as is customary with the Jesuits, embraced the classics, philosophy and the natural sciences. Teilhard had an aptitude for the latter, and when his turn came at the age of twenty-four to do the usual period as a 'scholastic' teacher in one of the schools of the Order, he was sent to Cairo to teach physics and chemistry. From 1905-8 he performed adequately in the classroom, though being only an amateur (as he called himself) in physics and chemistry he tended at times to talk above his pupils' heads. The mental discipline involved in the work must have been a powerful formative influence. Most of his leisure time in Egypt was spent out in the hills and desert searching for geological and palaeontological specimens, and for the rare insects that are a naturalist's delight. His *joie de vivre*, and his affection for his family, are finely expressed in his *Lettres d'Egypte 1905-1908*. He shows great confidence in the rightness of his pursuits, both secular and religious. In some of his descriptions, both of crowded street-scenes and of lonely desert and hills, he displays a literary quality that was later to form a splendid vehicle for his mystical works.

He communicated the results of his geological expeditions to

[6] Cuénot, *op. cit.*, p. 7.

professional bodies in Europe, and published a paper on *The Eocene Strata of the Minieh Region* in the Bulletin of the Egyptian Institute at Alexandria. By the time he was twenty-seven years of age, his name was known to professional colleagues, but if at this age one is on the verge of maturity in the secular world, a Jesuit is still very junior in the Order. Now began the customary period of four years' study of theology, for which he was sent to the house of study at Hastings. It is sometimes said that Teilhard's formal grounding in philosophy and theology was inadequate. Certainly he was not a 'professional' in either of these disciplines. In his essays and books he does not pepper his philosophical or theological assertions with scholarly references and quotations. The only medium in which he writes according to an established professional pattern is that of the formal scientific paper. Teilhard was always the scientist, constantly appealing to phenomena themselves for evidence of the truth of his conclusions. His philosophy and theology were 'new', but only in the sense that he reinterpreted ancient truths within the framework of scientific thought which alone makes any real sense to modern man. He was a missionary, exploring wholly new intellectual territory. Just because he does not use or quote the formulations of earlier philosophers or theologians one should not think that his Jesuit training had left him ignorant of them. Not long before he died he wrote ' . . . mounted as we are "on the shoulders" of Plato, Aristotle and St. Thomas . . .'. The expression seems to cause some surprise to his biographer Claude Cuénot.[7] But in fact the phrase, borrowed from a scientist's tribute to Newton and other predecessors, sums up succinctly a number of aspects of Teilhard which it might be convenient to list:

1. He was not a 'revolutionary' but rather an 'evolutionary'. That is, his thinking represents a genuine 'development of doctrine', wholly within the Christian tradition.
2. His experience of 'seeing further' than his predecessors led him to formulate his ideas in a wholly direct fashion.

[7] Cuénot, *op. cit.*, p. 13 n.

Conscious as he was of standing 'on the shoulders' of others, he could not use their language for recounting what they had not been tall enough to see. It is not the task of a pioneer of new thinking to draw comparisons with and make cross-references to the works of other pioneers. This can and should be left to the academics. There is every sign today that they are carrying out the assignment with vigour.

3. He was never a relativist where knowledge and thinking were concerned. Many of the debates of modern philosophers, like those of the later medieval schoolmen, he would have regarded as futile logic-chopping, interesting only in so far as they help to sharpen the wits, but fundamentally misguided in that they sometimes seem to imply that cleverness is all, and truth a phantom that always finally escapes detection.

4. In searching for truth and making it manifest to others he developed a system based on his scientific work. Just as an Einstein or a Darwin, in announcing a new hypothesis of great originality and generality, lets the internal coherence of the facts and the arguments speak for themselves, without constantly looking back over his shoulder to see how each new formulation 'squares' with earlier theories (most of which are often subsumed under the new one), so does Teilhard when giving voice to philosophical and theological insights of the deepest significance. If he does not quote continually this is not only because he mostly did his writing in remote places without access to original sources, but rather because he knew he had more important tasks to perform, and could safely leave the dotting of i's and the crossing of t's to others.

Priest and Mystic

He was ordained a priest in 1911, and after completing his final year of theology returned to France to undertake serious scientific study in geology and palaeontology. Even during his time at

Hastings he had continued with field-work where, as he later said, his 'chief passion was the Wealdian bone-beds and their fossil teeth content'. It was during that time that he came to know Sir Arthur Smith-Woodward professionally, and others connected with the British Museum. He maintained contact with British scientists throughout his life, and became quite fluent in the English language. But now in Paris it was with the great Marcellin Boule and the Abbé Breuil that his eyes were opened to the fascinating problems of the biological origin of man and his subsequent evolution. Apart from laboratory work with fossils he went on professional 'digs' with international teams of scientists (geologists, palaeontologists, palaeoanthropologists), and on explorations of the caves of prehistoric man in northern Spain. All the time, as priest and mystic, he was meditating the mystery of the incarnation that was re-enacted in his daily mass. What does it mean, to say that Christ came into the world as a personal saviour and redeemer of mankind? Did he redeem the men who had made the wall-paintings at Altamira? What about Neanderthal man, that other species of the same genus *homo*?

It was during this period that chance led Teilhard, during a visit to Hastings in August, 1913, to be drawn into a notorious hoax, carefully carried out over a period of three years, and now known as the Piltdown Forgery. During a visit to the Piltdown site with Smith-Woodward and Dawson, both of whom he had every reason to trust, he himself picked up a canine tooth of the 'dawn-man', which had been 'planted' there. The experience itself must have been emotionally rewarding. Perhaps it contributed to Teilhard's subsequent more passionate interest in human fossils rather than those of other genera. When the forgery was unmasked, forty years later, Teilhard wrote as follows to one of the 'detectives' who helped to solve the puzzle, Dr. K. P. Oakley of the British Museum,

I congratulate you most sincerely on your solution of the Piltdown problem. Anatomically speaking, 'Eoanthropus' was a kind of monster. And, from a palaeontological point of view, it was equally shocking that a 'dawn-Man' could occur in England. Therefore I am fundamentally pleased by your conclusions, in spite of the fact that, sentimentally speaking, it spoilt one of my brightest and earliest palaeontological memories.[8]

Wartime Experiences

When the First World War broke out it was some months before Teilhard was called to the colours. He had actually started his 'tertianship', back in a humble position in the seminary prior to making his solemn vows, when he was drafted as a non-combatant stretcher-bearer in the medical corps, attached to the Zouaves, and sent up to the front line. The next four years were crucial ones from the point of view of the development both of his personality and of his ideas. Still in the future were the experiences of the Far East, and all his scientific work as a fully fledged professional of international fame. But during his time in the trenches, between the ages of thirty-four and thirty-eight, he not only went through, with his soldier-colleagues, some of the deepest human experiences possible, but he welded his feelings for the earth, for his fellow-men, and for God, into a way of thinking that is already completely 'Teilhardian' in character.

There could be no better introduction to Teilhard than the two books which cover his wartime experiences. The first consists of the letters he wrote to his cousin Marguerite Teillard-Chambon, now published in translation as *The Making of a Mind: Letters from a Soldier-Priest*. The second, a book of his wartime essays, was first published in 1965 under the title *Écrits du Temps de la Guerre*. It is marvellously annotated by its editors, two old friends from the Jesuit Order, and is printed with full ecclesiastical approval. These are important points. As with quite a lot that Teilhard wrote, some of these essays were not intended by him for publication;[9] some of them were 'trial runs', written to get his ideas

---

[8] Cuénot, *op. cit.*, p. 21.

[9] See *Letters from a Traveller* (Collins), p. 206, for example, for his attitude to an essay 'strictly limited in intention to some intimate friends in my own profession' (i.e. religious).

straight, or written for the critical comments of friends and colleagues. So great has been the impact of Teilhard de Chardin since his death that virtually everything that he ever wrote is likely now to be published. It is therefore very important, in reading him, to be able to 'place' the particular work, and to know what degree of importance he himself attached to it. Of the wartime essays now available in print he submitted only two for publication. One was refused, the other (*La Nostalgie du Front*) was published in the Jesuit journal *Études*, but shorn of its final paragraph in which he compared the awful splendour of the front line to other catastrophic spectacles during the course of evolution, of which the only spectators had been animals without reflective powers. The comparison of himself, witness of the Front of war, with such an animal just beginning to realise what was happening, must have been too much for the ecclesiastical censor, and it was cut.

Teilhard later said that there was nothing in his wartime essays that he had not subsequently said at greater length and with more precision. But they form an indispensable stepping-stone to his more advanced works, where at times his passion for neologisms, and the dexterity with which he mingles scientific, poetical and mystical insights, become somewhat confusing. What is truly astonishing, both about the essays and the letters written at this period, is that they could have been composed at all under the circumstances of trench warfare. Like all the rest, he was periodically under fire during an engagement, and then moved back for recuperative purposes. His job as a stretcher-bearer was physically arduous and emotionally demanding. He refused promotion to officer rank as chaplain, but was always ready to give spiritual comfort as a priest, as well as medical comfort, to the wounded. He served throughout as a corporal, and his bravery under fire won him the Croix de Guerre, the Médaille Militaire and the Chevalier du Légion d'Honneur.

His mind seems always to have been at work. During lulls in the fighting he would be writing one of his spiritual essays; or drafting a scientific thesis on geological strata that he studied in the walls of the trenches themselves; or meditating on the condition of man and his relationship with God; or helping an overworked parish priest in a village behind the lines; or writing to his cousin those comforting and consoling letters that speak so highly of his powers as a spiritual director and a man of God who had great warmth of feeling.

One gets the impression that the experience of the First World War set the seal on Teilhard's maturing. The essays that he wrote, often under great strain, and suffering from physical fatigue, show him hammering out his sense of the cosmic, and of the rôle of the cosmic Christ, ideas which were to be ever deepened during the next forty years. It is almost unbelievable that these insights, expressed in a warm vibrant style that is always under control despite the passionate love for God and all his creation, should have emanated from the mud and weariness of the trenches in the First World War. That they could do so are evidence of three important features of Teilhard's life: first, the wholeness and integrity of his personality that stemmed from childhood; secondly, the fundamental optimism that came from his deep trust in God and in God's creative work in the universe: it was this that allowed him to extract from the horrors of war the spiritual benefits that could accrue to its participants if only they would open themselves and work for them; and thirdly, the sheer discipline of mind and body that came from the long years of training in the Jesuit Order. His cousin reported that sometimes his handwriting would be shaky, showing signs of strain. His thought, however, remained always firm, calm and confident.

Professional Scientist

On demobilisation in March, 1919 Teilhard went back to being a student, and worked for a degree in Natural Sciences at the Sorbonne. All examinations passed within a year, he started research work, under Boule at the Museum, for his doctoral thesis. He chose as his subject *The Mammals of the Lower Eocene Period in France* (that is, the earliest mammalian forms to evolve, some

70–100 million years ago, following on the 'age of reptiles'). The thesis gained high praise from the jury which, in the words of the official report,[10] 'did not hesitate a moment in granting him the title of doctor with very honourable mention'. The report also stated that the candidate was 'certainly destined for a fine scientific future'. The year 1922 saw the publication of his doctoral thesis and two scientific papers. He was awarded prizes both by the Geological Society of France and the Academy of Sciences, and was appointed lecturer in Geology at the Institut Catholique.

It is common enough in France, though rare in England, for priests to have secular appointments in academic fields. Teilhard was by now living the life of a fully professional scientist, researching, publishing, lecturing, in contact with fellow-scientists both at home and abroad. He was also living a full priestly life, preaching, saying mass, conducting retreats, and deepening his spiritual insights by meditation and writing. An important essay dating from 1921 was entitled (in translation) *Science and Christ (or analysis and synthesis). Remarks on how the scientific study of matter can and should serve to lift one to the divine centre*. The development of his views was made possibly by his complete acceptance of what his own scientific studies had shown him to be beyond question, namely that the world is a world in evolution. He saw man as a part of the evolutionary process, a part that is on the main axis of what has been a progressive phenomenon, a true 'development', throughout time. In such a framework of thought the old dualism of mind and matter, observer and observed, that has bedevilled both science and philosophy ever since the start of the modern scientific era, vanished 'like fog before rising sun' for Teilhard.

If we seem to have spent an inordinate amount of the limited space available on the chronicle of Teilhard's early life, this is because of the present writer's belief that by the time of his first visit to the Far East in 1923, to China where his greatest work was to be done, the main strands of Teilhard's thought had already

[10] Quoted Cuénot, *op. cit.*, p. 30.

been clearly defined. Aged forty-two, he was in the prime of life, though 'young' still in the Jesuit Order. He had reached many daring conclusions in his attempts to penetrate the mystery of being, many daring 'solutions' to the problems facing the church in a post-Christian world where science, in a framework of agnostic humanism, was clearly in the ascendancy. Teilhard was wholly sympathetic toward developments in science, and toward those aspects of service to humanity in which anti-religious movements appeared to have gained the initiative. He saw his life's work as that of an apostle to scientists, though not as preacher or proselyte because that sort of approach was anathema to scientists including himself. An apostle, though, who by his own life and work would show that the old antagonisms between the respect for truth as shown in fields of scientific progress, and the respect for truth as shown in adherence to religious traditions, had been the result of exaggerations and misconceptions. Not for Teilhard the attitude of those 'believing' scientists who shed their religion as they enter the laboratory. But one need not say or do anything that was not wholly scientific in form and temper; indeed it was vital to stick to the deductive rules of science, and the principle of verification of both hypotheses and deductions. All this constituted progress in thinking and understanding, and was therefore fundamentally religious in nature. As Teilhard was to say much later, 'Everything that rises must converge.'

China

The invitation from a fellow-Jesuit, Father Licent, to come to China for a year to assist in geological and palaeontological excavations, was wholly natural and fitting at this stage in his career. Licent had already spent ten years exploring the basin of the Yellow River, building up collections of specimens for the local museum he founded. He had already had help from Boule and Teilhard, at the Paris Museum, in identification of fossil mammals. In 1923 he invited Teilhard to join him in field work.

This first experience of the Orient really put some of Teilhard's insights to the test. In an early letter from China he says,

> As a tentative summary, I may say that from the rapid view I have had of so many different kinds of people since I left Marseilles I retain above all the impression that the world is much more vast and more formidably complicated than I ever thought. Really, a journey to the Far East seems to represent a sort of 'temptation of the multiple'.[11] How can one hope for the unification in mind and in heart of so many fragmentations of mankind, embracing every stage from savagery to a neo-civilisation appreciably at variance with our Christian outlook?
>
> I am persuaded that at all costs we must cling to a faith in *some direction* and in *some destination* assignable to all this restless human activity (27 May, 1923).[12]

It was during this first visit to China, in the Ordos Desert where there was 'neither bread, nor wine, nor altar', that he composed one of his most beautiful meditations, *La Messe sur le Monde*. This again is a working out in fuller form and detail of the wartime essay 'Le Prêtre', of which one of his Jesuit superiors had warmly approved and another had doubts ('very affectionately though', as he told his cousin). *The Mass Upon the World* is unquestionably a spiritual classic, which shows an appreciation of the full significance of the incarnation, and is expressed in superb poetical form. At the time of composing it he was spending his days, it should be remembered, in grubbing about in the earth for rocks and fossils. Once again he himself is the living embodiment of his most advanced thought.

During their first expedition, Teilhard and Licent made the important discovery of traces of Palaeolithic Man in China. They were able to bring back with them large quantities of ancient worked stone, for study during the winter months. Teilhard also made contact in Peking with international scholars, especially

[11] An essay of 1917 had been entitled 'La Lutte contre la multitude': it is published in *Ecrits du Temps de la Guerre*.

[12] Cuénot, *op. cit.*, p. 45.

American. He wrote home to France many letters showing his acute powers of observation, his accurate assessments of men and situations, and above all a 'philanthropy' large enough to overcome an initially strong dislike of the Chinese and their ways of life. He had enjoyed an experience of the East which had widened his horizons still further. But he was keen to return to the intellectual life of Paris, and to the libraries and museums of Europe.

Back in Europe

Between 1924 and 1926 he wrote and published a large number of important scientific papers on the observations he had made in China. He kept up his contacts with England and Belgium, and developed, to an intense degree, his ideas on the implications of evolution, in regular Wednesday-evening discussions with Édouard le Roy of the Collège de France. It was during this period that Teilhard coined, with le Roy, the term 'noosphere' to represent the gradual development, with the evolution of man, of a 'thinking layer' around the world. In 1925 he wrote an essay the title of which (in translation) includes other expressions that have made his name so well known in recent years: 'Hominization. Introduction to a scientific study of the phenomenon of man.' At the same time Teilhard was giving talks and retreats to students in Paris, and was developing very daring interpretations, for instance, of the doctrine of original sin. He is known, too, to have given a very sympathetic interpretation (in terms of Christian spirituality) of André Gide's *Les Nourritures terrestres*. His speculations about, and interpretations of, the scientific significance of human evolution or 'hominization', were recorded largely by le Roy, both in public lectures and in books, where he repeatedly quoted Teilhard in order to acknowledge his debt to him. So far as the development of his theology was concerned he was, at this time, writing and perfecting his greatest single work *Le Milieu Divin* which, although completed in 1927, and despite the efforts of many friends both inside and outside the circles of ecclesiastical authority, failed to be published until thirty years

later, two years after Teilhard's death. In a later chapter the
dangers of pantheism which scared the authorities will be referred to. It is clear that during this period in Europe, when
Teilhard was free to lecture and preach about the spiritual insights that had been granted him, the excitement and enthusiasm
that he provoked made him a man to be watched very carefully
by his superiors in religion. Could one have a Jesuit openly
approving of agnostic humanists like Gide on the literary side
and H. G. Wells on the 'popular science' side? His supporters
among the intelligentsia would make copies of transcriptions of
lectures he had given, and of essays he had written (often without
his approval or authority, and sometimes with variations creeping
into the text – a hazard which can create untold difficulties for
anyone who tries, like Teilhard, to walk an intellectual tightrope).

If there appears to be a certain *naïveté* in his outspokenness
during a markedly anti-modernist, conservative phase in the
attitude of Rome, this is absolutely in keeping with his position
as a great pioneer of thought. It indicates three aspects of his
character which it is well always to bear in mind. First, he was
completely without fear. This he had demonstrated clearly
enough, so far as life itself was concerned, during the war. He
was equally intrepid on the intellectual 'front', fighting against
the complacent, reactionary and intransigent 'establishment' of
orthodox ecclesiology. 'We must dare all', he was fond of saying
in later life. Secondly, he was superbly confident that, however
hard he and others might have to wrestle with words and ideas
to get his fundamental vision properly expressed, nevertheless it
was the right one, and therefore orthodox in the proper meaning
of the term. He could, in consequence, set out on the tightrope,
even above a Niagara Falls of heresy-sniffing theologians, confident that however many alarms there might be *en route* he would
reach the other side in safety. 'I go towards him who comes' –
like Peter walking over the waves to his master. Teilhard was
especially fond of this gospel story. Thirdly, we see evidence of
his complete integrity. A man who tries to produce a synthesis
of ideas drawn from modern science as well as from the Bible and

the early Fathers, drawn both from the laboratory and from the spiritual treasury of two thousand years of Christian prayer and thought, is bound to be beset with temptations to compromise in order to make his message more palatable to this group or that. The furthest that Teilhard would go in that sort of thing is exemplified by an extract from a letter written while he was trying to get permission from Rome to publish *The Phenomenon of Man* in 1948–49:

> On reflection, I thought the best way was to satisfy the censor's demands, without any distortion, of course, of my thought, but by going through the text dotting the i's and crossing the t's (in footnotes, and also in the dozen pages, which are now ready, of epilogue, which seems to me useful). I think these re-touchings have improved my original draft.[13]

These are the words of an honest man blessed with the virtue of prudence, not those of a political schemer trying to hoodwink the church into accepting something incompatible with her divinely-inspired heritage. That he was fully conscious both of his own position and of likely misinterpretations of it, is shown in another letter[14] from the same period. He was discussing, as so often, the 'faith in heaven' and the 'faith in earth' which he saw to be essential to the realisation by Christians and all men of the doctrine of the mystical body:

> The synthesis of the two forms of faith in *Christo Jesu* is not an arbitrarily chosen tactical move *ad usum infidelium*. It represents *hic et nunc* a condition of survival for an increasing number of Christians. We have to choose right now between the Christianising of neo-humanism and its condemnation. The problem is with us now, and time is short.

But Rome was not quite ready, in 1949, for the *aggiornamento* for which Teilhard, perhaps, has been as much responsible as John XXIII. He was refused permission not only to publish *The*

---

[13] *Letters from a Traveller*, p. 301.
[14] Quoted Cuénot, *op. cit.*, p. 271.

Phenomenon of Man, but also to accept the highest academic position that France could offer, that of Professor at the Collège de France. Disappointed and sad, but not unduly downhearted, he said *à propos* his continuing to send to friends, as he was allowed, copies of unpublished writings,

> I have decided to continue as before, trusting to the good fortune, or rather, the legitimacy of my cause. I know that that is what all the heretics said. But, for the most part, they did not take up their position solely to exalt Christ above all things: and, basically, that is the only charge that can be brought against me.[15]

Others who seek, these days, to 'bring Christianity up to date' by the jettisoning of established doctrine, and in pursuit of contemporary fashions (temporary only, precisely because they are 'contemporary') destroy the foundations of the Christian religion, would benefit by studying carefully the life and works of this Jesuit scientist who was maligned at times by some as the archheretic of the age. His acceptance of the restrictions imposed on him, his loyalty and obedience to those in authority over him, and his abiding faith nevertheless that one day his views would be shared not merely by the Church of Rome but by all men of goodwill, represent an object-lesson to us all.

Exile

We jumped from the 1920's to the 1940's in order to illustrate Teilhard's reaction to 'defeat' when he had been trying hard to get his most famous work approved by the ecclesiastical censors. He had shown himself, from the days of earliest maturity, to be aware of the nature and strength of the opposition to his views that he was inevitably to contend with. Despite all the frustrations of censorship and the fact that decisions were often made by nameless officials in Rome, and given without explanation or rational argument, Teilhard never allowed himself to become

[15] Quoted Cuénot, *op. cit.*, p. 272.

unduly distressed and rebellious. It was as if his understanding
of the evolutionary process made him realise that time was on
his side.

He might well have thought himself, in the 1920's, to be
permanently settled (except that a Jesuit is never that) in Paris, a
fully-committed 'worker-priest' in the academic milieu. But his
influence on the young was regarded as too dangerous. Parisian
students have always been intensely interested in ideas, and are
naturally prone to be *avant-garde*: the young priest-scientist who
never shrank from facing any question squarely and honestly was
something of a hero to them, and they copied and distributed his
essays in a way that was bound to disturb his religious superiors.
Teilhard received instructions (sympathetically given) that he
must concentrate on scientific work and must return to China for
this purpose. Decisions were made and conveyed to him in
stages. The equanimity with which he accepted them is shown in
a letter written from China at the beginning of 1927,

> . . . your letter of December 5 reached me only this morning,
> with its news that my connection with the Institut Catholique
> has been definitely severed. I am little affected by this news.
> When I left Paris in April it was with the impression that my
> future was wholly uncertain; and I have since lived in China
> with the growing feeling that in this country I have found a
> new home. So, you see, the break with my way of life from
> 1920 to 1926 was in some regards already complete.[16]

Of course France was always 'home' to Teilhard. He was
always glad to return, and was sad for this among other, deeper
reasons, when the Second World War kept him away for some
years. But it would be quite wrong to think of him as 'pining
away' in exile. No Jesuit does that. Teilhard's own philosophy
led him to become a 'citizen of the world', completely at home
in any part of it in which he happened to find himself. This involved no cutting of ties, or repudiation of roots. In his anthro-

[16] Quoted Cuénot, *op. cit.*, p. 63.

pological theories of race he was wholly opposed to the policy
of 'miscegenation'. He wanted every racial group to be conscious
of and proud of its history and of its special qualities and attributes, and yet to transcend 'racialism' in recognising a greater
loyalty to the whole human race and the cosmos out of which it
has arisen. Teilhard never allowed himself to appear the mis-
understood, downtrodden martyr-figure that some have tried to
make him out to be. Whatever some of his devotees may seem
to indicate about themselves, he himself showed no trace of
paranoia.

And so he accepted, in 1926–27, what some have called his
'banishment' to China with calm assurance and good humour.
China offered him limitless scope for exploring the scientific
problem of early man, and it was essential to his philosophical
and theological ideas that they should be firmly rooted in the
phenomena themselves. This meant that he must at all costs keep
his feet on the ground, and follow the evidence wherever it may
lead, confident that if only he was true to himself and to the facts,
the road of truth would be bound ultimately to lead to its divine
author. The honest, humble, and objective search for truth has
been the hallmark of great scientists down the ages. Teilhard is
one of their number.

His scientific exploits in the Far East during the dozen years
that preceded the start of the Second World War are fully re-
counted in Cuénot's indispensable biography. In addition, two
of his scientific colleagues of the period, George B. Barbour[17]
and Helmut de Terra[18] have written books about their experiences with him. In this branch of science colleagues are bound to
get to know one another unusually well. Field expeditions in
geology and palaeontology are carried out in circumstances
which are often very trying: small travelling groups may be
trekking for weeks in the remotest corners of the globe, sleeping
under canvas, prepared to endure extremes of climate and

[17] George B. Barbour, *In the Field with Teilhard de Chardin* (Herder and
Herder, New York, 1965).
[18] Helmut de Terra, *Memories of Teilhard de Chardin* (Collins).

C

comfort if the need arises. A man is unlikely to be able to conceal his true personality for long in such conditions. Everyone who knew him has testified (whatever his own religion or lack of it) to Teilhard's worth not only as a scientist but also as a man, and also (but only when he was specifically invited to draw on his spiritual experience) as a priest.

His work of scientific exploration with international research teams, especially the integral part he played in the discovery at Choukoutien of *Pithecanthropus*, that close cousin of *Homo sapiens* who lived in China a quarter of a million years ago, led to the publication, over the years, of a great many scientific articles of quality. It was these that later brought him the highest academic distinctions. For these he was universally renowned and respected within the sober circle of his scientific peers.

The massive bibliography of Teilhard's works, published as an appendix to Cuenot's biography, lists all these publications, in order of writing or of appearance. Among them there are listed each year an essay or two with titles such as, 'Le sens humain', 'Christologie et évolution', 'Comment je crois', 'Quelques réflexions sur la conversion du monde'. Needless to say these were not written for immediate publication. Some of them are still waiting, and will appear in the last two of the eleven projected volumes of Collected Works, of which nine have so far been published.

It may even have been that Teilhard was consciously writing these essays for posthumous publication. Soon after the start of his extended period in China he wrote as follows concerning his profound spiritual work, *Le Milieu divin*, which he had been urged to publish, if possible, for the benefit of others,

> On my return from the trip I found a letter from Louvain from Père Charles) telling me that my manuscript on *Le Milieu divin* was to be printed without delay (about 5 July), 'all the opinions having been favourable'. Since then, no news. I am beginning to think that there may have been a hitch – and almost feel relieved (I put so much of my own self into those

pages that I might prefer them to appear posthumously) (6 December, 1929).[19]

It is natural for a writer, like any creative artist, to want to see his work published, to feel he is communicating his thoughts to others. Teilhard undoubtedly went through periods of crisis and mental anguish, especially in earlier years, about the restrictions imposed on his freedom in these matters, and later when, with the publication of the papal encyclical *Humani generis* (1950), he felt that the reactionaries had gained ground and would prevent his own writings from ever seeing the light of day. And yet he survived with his loyalty untarnished, and with his faith in God, the church, his Order and himself as firm as ever. If his greatest works were to appear only posthumously, then perhaps he could feel even freer in the writing of them. The only real urgency he felt was that of an apostle who wanted to make it possible for the gospel to reach again to the mind and heart of modern man. If this could not come about until after his death (his 'change of state') the delay was a small one in comparison with the age of the church, and an infinitely small one on that other canvas on which Teilhard was accustomed to seeing mankind, the history of a world in evolution.

It is well known that ecclesiastical opponents of Teilhard's ideas both in Rome and elsewhere have voiced their objections to some purpose. The *Monitum* decree of 1962 warned bishops and heads of seminaries of the dangers thought to be inherent in Teilhard's writings. Many of us had feared much worse than a 'warning' from the Holy Office that did not, significantly enough, carry the signature of the Pope. It should be remembered that the writings of St. Thomas Aquinas (bulwark of orthodoxy, as he has been thought of for centuries) were actually condemned for some thirty years after his death. So it is with all pioneers of new ways of thinking about God and his dealings with men. The original deposit of faith enshrined in the New Testament must not be dissipated or harmed in any way, but only enriched by an ever

[19] Quoted Cuénot, *op. cit.*, p. 118.

deeper understanding. The initial judgment as to whether a new formulation represents an enrichment or a dissipation is a human one, and is subject to all the frailties, both psychological and spiritual, to which individual men are prone.

It would not have been surprising if the works of Teilhard, forbidden publication during his life, had been formally condemned after his death pending their detailed scrutiny by appointed experts. The chances of formal condemnation have grown more and more remote as the years have gone by. His name has been openly praised in the Vatican Council, and by individual prelates and members of the Jesuit Order (including the newly-elected Father General of the Society) in various parts of the world. But clearly the projected Volume XI of his collected works will contain some of the most far-reaching and controversial essays from the theological point of view. The projected title is *Christianisme et évolution*, and the volume will contain essays from all periods from 1920 (including one from that year on the doctrine of the 'fall' of man) to 1955, when his last completed essay bore the fitting title *Recherche, travail et adoration*.

This digression on the problems of publication was intended to indicate something of the atmosphere in which Teilhard 'lived and divinised' (to use a phrase of his) the last thirty years or so of his life. Throughout that time he worked extremely hard in the cause of science, and travelled extensively between Europe and the Far East, America and Africa, in order to do field work, attend conferences, visit friends and colleagues, and above all to develop his 'sense of earth' *pari passu* with the development of his 'sense of heaven'. During the Second World War his movements were restricted because of the Japanese invasion of China. It was during the early part of this enforced immobility that he wrote his most famous book, *The Phenomenon of Man*.

After 1945

After the war he returned to Paris where, for a period of five years, he engaged in many typical activities of a highly respected *savant*. His work was interrupted by a heart attack in 1947 which left him permanently weakened physically, but robust as ever intellectually. He contributed to conferences and discussions, both scientific and philosophico-theological, but he had to respect his superiors' instructions that there was to be no repetition of the kind of influence he had had on large audiences of Parisian students in the period following the First World War. He took part in debates with philosophers like Marcel and Berdiaeff, Lavelle and Hyppolite (a student of Heidegger). During this period he seems to have established or re-established contact with many branches of intellectual life, and to have begun to concentrate more and more on the future of man rather than on his remote past. He took part in the discussions of UNESCO, and got to know well its director, Sir Julian Huxley.

The two became firm friends because, although their fundamental philosophies were so different, nevertheless, because they had each tried to understand 'the phenomenon of man' as a scientific exercise, they had arrived at remarkably similar conclusions as to the paths that lay open to man for his future psycho-social evolution. He began to make ambitious plans for research in the field of human energetics, conceived of as a natural science. At the same time he was continuing to write his 'opuscules' and was engaged, of course, in those negotiations with Rome of which mention was made earlier. Rome's double refusal (*a*) to allow his name to go forward for the chair at the Collège de France and (*b*) to allow his book to be published, were bitter blows. Not that he sought his own advancement. But the first would have given him the right kind of 'platform' from which to launch his epoch-making book. These rebuttals, coupled with his Order's insistence that he leave Paris yet again, and for what he feared would be the last time, made him, for a time in 1951, at the age of seventy, a rather sad and lonely figure. This was when he asked a friend, 'Pray for me, that I may not die embittered.'

But depression never lasted long with Teilhard. From Paris he was off to South Africa to see for himself the remains of those astonishing pre-human primates known as *Australopithecinae*, upright, plain-dwelling creatures who lived over a million years ago and some of whom (it is now known, though it was not at the time Teilhard was there) knew the use of tools. His far-ranging mind was busy drawing up a plan for organised research to be undertaken by the Wenner-Gren Foundation, on whose behalf he was acting. Apart from a second visit to South Africa in 1953 he spent the remaining years of his life in America, mostly working in the Headquarters of this Foundation as one of their Research Fellows. His productivity remained unimpaired, each year seeing the completion of ten or a dozen articles, of which the scientific ones were published in the normal way and the others, containing some of his most profound formulations of the world 'ahead' converging steadily on to God 'on high', are included in one or other of the volumes of Collected Works.

His life on earth concluded in the way that was sketched in the Introduction. It was a noble life, full of interest, and indeed fascination, for people of all kinds. His impact was considerable during his life, and now it is proving to be enormous. At once a 'child of heaven and son of earth' he was exactly the example needed to show the modern restless world how to find the way ahead.

2

Thought

TEILHARD's thinking is based throughout on his practical knowledge of phenomena-in-themselves, and the deductions that must logically be drawn from them. This is as true for his mystical writings as it is for his work in natural science. He writes what he does because this is what he has seen, what he has experienced, what, after exercising his disciplined mind on the experience, he *knows*. It is this that gives his prose its freshness and urgency. His style is at times highly complex, at times simple and direct, at times pure poetry of the highest quality. But his thought stays always close to the phenomena and the conclusions they suggest.

In this short book the reader has been introduced to a number of aspects of Teilhard's thinking in the somewhat extended biographical section. This method of presentation was chosen deliberately in order to emphasise the different quality one meets in Teilhard compared with many writers. Much philosophical and theological writing seems wholly divorced from the life and personality of its author, sometimes divorced from the realities of living altogether. Such books stand alone like orphans: gifted, specialised offspring of unknown parents. They make their appeal entirely within the restricted framework of the particular discipline (or part of it) concerned. This feature is sometimes held to be the hallmark of true scholarship, and a sure guarantee of the author's worth and significance. But it is just such specialisation that leads direct to the modern tower of Babel. Analysis gets lost in its own ramifications if it is not accompanied by synthesis. If it is easy for anyone to miss the wood for the trees, what is likely to be the position of one who spends all his time studying branches and twigs, and never sees even the individual tree of which they form a part? Teilhard the thinker cannot be divorced from Teilhard the man, and Teilhard the man was both practical man of science and mystic, whose complementary qualities we have attempted to indicate in the previous chapter.

Evolution

The theme that runs through all his writing is that of *genesis* or becoming. For this insight into the nature of a process which he saw operative everywhere, his scientific work as a student of biological evolution was absolutely fundamental. It is true, of course, that he was not the first to formulate some of the problems posed by the nineteenth-century discovery of evolution. But he was the first to grasp the immensity of the change in thinking to which this discovery must give rise, and he was the first to enunciate, both in general outline and at times in great detail, what the Christian message really means in the light of this shattering new insight into the nature of things.

Only a relatively small number of people have actually grasped the implications or even the fact of the scientific theory of evolution. One is not thinking so much of those back-woodsmen who speak of evolution as though it were 'a mere scientific theory', therefore corrigible and even, possibly, quite false. They have nearly all disappeared, except perhaps from some of the fastnesses of the Roman curia. One is thinking rather of those churchmen who blithely say they have no difficulty in accepting the theory of evolution, and in incorporating it into their Christian way of life, when they clearly show they have little grasp of what the theory really means. For them, one suspects, evolution is really only one small branch of the biological sciences, that need cause no more disturbance than, say, the valency-theory in chemistry. For Teilhard, who saw with the eyes of a professional, 'Evolution is a light illuminating all facts, a curve that all lines must follow.'[20] This is no hyperbole. He goes on, in the same passage,

What makes and classifies a 'modern' man (and a whole host of our contemporaries is not yet 'modern' in this sense) is

[20] *The Phenomenon of Man*, p. 219.

having become capable of seeing in terms not of space and time alone, but also of duration, or – and it comes to the same thing – of biological space-time; and above all having become incapable of seeing anything otherwise – anything – *not even himself*.

The reason why it is so difficult even for modern sophisticated man to think in terms of 'biological space-time' (the significance of 'biological' added to the more usual phrase 'space-time', is that this implies a *direction* which Einsteinian space-time lacks), is that such a concept contradicts all the ordinary, everyday, 'common-sense' information that we are equipped to receive. The Copernican theory appeared to contradict not only all common-sense knowledge about the way the ground stayed still under one's feet, but also the highly-sophisticated observations and deductions of the Ptolemaic astronomers and mathematicians. Similarly the general theory of evolution appears to contradict all common-sense 'knowledge' of how things seem to stay much the same or, if they do change, do so in a cyclical fashion – which means, in the end, that things are static. From time immemorial this is how the world has been seen. A static or cyclical nature seems an inevitable consequence of the ordinary, unaided observations such as each of us is capable of making during his limited life-span. Cyclical views of history, such as those of Spengler or Toynbee, represent a slightly wider range of insight, but are still conditioned by this static view of the world that is virtually universal. Such views, against which Teilhard battled unceasingly, are so deeply ingrained in our conscious and unconscious minds, that they have affected all branches of knowledge, including philosophy and theology. Because they lead men, in the end, to despise a physical world which never gets anywhere, they have been manipulated by 'spiritistic' writers of all religions in order to persuade the faithful to concentrate on an extrinsic, transcedent 'God on high', and neglect not only the intrinsic, immanent 'God within' but also, as we learn to say with Teilhard, the 'God ahead'.

Taken to its logical conclusions such neglect of the immanent Godhead has always led to formal heresy: manicheeism, albigensianism, jansenism, puritanism. And even when kept within bounds it tends to produce an emasculated theology which cannot really give an adequate account of the incarnation and redemption, except in terms of reparation for the fall of a mythical Adam and Eve who lived perfect lives in the Garden of Eden. Modern man will rightly have none of that. Where then are St. Paul's two Adams, the one bringing pain and suffering, the other redemption and joy? Are we to abandon Paul? That is why professional theologians are wary of Teilhard.

It is not only Christians who have naturally thought in terms of a static, cyclical or 'fixist' world. We all do it, all the time. Even after the Copernican revolution, science itself was thoroughly 'fixist' in its understanding of the world. Linnaeus could not have invented his binomial system of nomenclature, indicating genus and species, unless he had believed completely in the doctrine of the fixity of species. Opposition to Darwin's theory of evolution came first from scientists, not from theologians. So it had been with Copernicus three hundred years earlier. Most adult people have a natural psychological tendency toward conservatism in major matters, and show a natural wariness toward dynamic theories, preferring usually the static and unimaginative. The same natural preference for 'sameness' rather than 'newness' has drawn the sting out of the evolutionary concept itself: after the last century's optimism about evolutionary progress and advance, theorists of the twentieth century have mostly settled for a cyclical, static and ultimately meaningless 'evolutionary' process, one in which there is constant change but no 'direction' in any significant sense. One cannot but think that much of this sort of 'scientific' theory has been developed in response to philosophical pressures. The leading biologists in the early days of evolutionary theory were agnostics like Haeckel and Huxley. Out of loyalty to them, later scientists pursued their philosophical predilections to the point where all meaning was taken out of the concept of evolution, now conceived of as a random process that produces rises and falls in equal numbers and proportions, a process that will end when at last all energy-differentials have come to rest in a world grown cold and lifeless.

A profound pessimism lurks at the bottom of all purely mechanistic theories of the universe. This influence has been felt by all who have had the courage to face it ever since the start of the modern scientific era. It was never shown more clearly than by H. G. Wells, prophet of progress, whose last work was entitled *Mind at the End of its Tether*. The most mechanistic field of science today is biology, where simple nineteenth-century concepts of the nature of the physical universe for the most part hold sway. It is a curious situation when, at a time when fundamental physics is making enormous headway in theory, the science of biology still operates as though the mechanistic, 'billiard-ball' concept of matter, was true for all time. On this basis biological evolution is the chance product of random events which 'move' things this way or that solely according to statistical averages. The human mind itself is the result of the operation of such chance events, and is ultimately as futile and meaningless as anything else in this kaleidoscopic world. Charles Darwin saw the problem clearly, as he did most problems, and wrote.[21] 'But then arises the doubt, can the mind of man, which has, as I fully believe, been developed from a mind as low as that possessed by the lowest animal, be trusted when it draws such grand conclusions?'

The self-doubts and self-hates of modern man are one of the results of tying biology to out-of-date physical laws. Ultimately the theory is self-defeating because there is no meaning to be attached to 'meaning'. The Christian reacts either by ignoring the problem, or by retreating into a fundamentalism that is wholly anti-intellectual, or by putting his trust in an 'existential' encounter with God. The agnostic or atheistic existentialist has nothing but himself and other 'absurdities' in an absurd world to fall back on. If he is honest, he finds himself, as Sartre did, with the 'Nausea'.[22]

[21] *Autobiography*, 1876.
[22] *La Nausée*, Paris, 1938. Penguin translation, 1965.

Teilhard cuts clean through an outlook based on a misunderstanding of science, and appeals directly to the facts displayed by his own sciences of geology and palaeontology. Ever since our earth was formed, not less than five and probably not more than ten thousand million years ago, it has displayed a unidirectional trend. True, we cannot say (and by the nature of things cannot know) whether the world, or indeed the whole universe of matter, was preceded by one or a series of other universes. It may be that the process is cyclical at that level. But within the fantastically long time-scale of our present universe there can be no doubt, according to Teilhard, that events have occurred along a unidirectional axis. Minor axes have developed at all stages, like branches from a tree. The tree continues to grow and flourish, and its topmost shoot, in the axis of the trunk, is the essential 'growing-point'.[23]

Teilhard's key concept is what he called the 'Law of Complexity-Consciousness.' This will in due course become known, as is customary in science, as 'Teilhard's Law.' The law states two things:

1. Throughout time there has been a tendency in evolution for matter to become increasingly complex in its organisation.

2. With increase in material complexity there is a corresponding rise in the consciousness of the matter (or organism as it eventually becomes).

Consciousness is not something imported or injected into matter, it is one of its fundamental properties or 'faces'. The process of complexification comes about through an internal propensity of matter to unite. This is a feature of the physical world hitherto largely ignored by scientists, who have concentrated on analysis of another tendency discernible in the

[23] His discernment of this growing-point as Man is far from being the result of simple anthropocentrism. It is worked out with rigorous logic. It looks to a future full of promise both for mankind and for the church of Christ. The 'promise' is no self-deluding pious hope, but is a legitimate extrapolation from the facts, a prediction based on a hypothesis which is truly scientific because capable of being either verified or proved false.

universe, that of organised matter to disintegrate, to break up, become more random, more dispersed. Teilhard distinguishes this long-recognised form of energy, in which there is a 'natural' flow from less probable to more probable states (and which forms the basis of the laws of thermodynamics) as 'tangential energy'. But there is another form of natural energy, which leads to a build-up of 'stored complexity', from the building-bricks of hydrogen (or rather its component sub-atomic particles) to the staggering organisation that is self-reflective man (or even Christ, who was also a man and was also made of matter). This Teilhard calls 'radial energy'. Out of primitive chaos, order has come by the operation of natural laws. Until now scientists have spent their time reducing complexity to simpler forms of organisation. Every successful analysis has been welcomed as an 'explanation' of the complex that had been taken to pieces. It is not surprising that the enterprise looked like ending up with the random movements of atoms: chaos and the void. We have been naïve to a degree. A new era for scientists, as both analysers and synthesisers, is beginning. We must now learn how 'radial energy' operates. The rules of scientific evidence and verification will be as strict as ever. But science will wear a different face. It will have taken a great step forward.

Radial Energy

Ever since it was established that the earth is a sphere, certain words have been used to emphasise its 'sphericity'. The most commonly used is 'atmosphere' to denote the envelope of gas that surrounds the earth's crust. The molten interior of the earth is known to scientists as the 'barysphere' (though as yet relatively little is known about its composition and the forces under which it operates). The hard crust is known as the 'lithosphere', and the layer of water which covers most of its surface, and which alternates between lithosphere and atmosphere by evaporation and subsequent condensation, is known as the 'hydrosphere'. It was almost certainly in this intermediate watery layer that the

D

further complexification of inorganic matter went on during the thousands (probably) of millions of years that preceded the emergence of any organisation that could be called 'living'. It is in order to account for this build-up, long before 'natural selection' began to operate as a mechanism that would guarantee the survival of more complex forms, that Teilhard postulated his 'radial energy' in matter, an energy seeking union, a dynamic force inherent in physical structure, which eventually manifests itself as love.

Is this force blind or purposeful? By a characteristic stroke of genius Teilhard hits on an expression which satisfies observations that have led others always to come down on either the one side or the other, and hurl abuse at those in the opposite camp. The evolutionary process, whether at the pre-life stage, or throughout biological evolution, and even (for the most part) when, with the development of self-reflective consciousness in man, it could and should become consciously purposeful, he describes as a 'groping' process. Groping movements are 'random' until the 'purpose' is achieved, and then they go to work on the next phase.

The term 'biosphere' was coined in the first decade of this century[24] in order to denote that 'living layer' around the earth which has developed within and from, and has subsequently spread throughout, a very narrow inorganic layer made up of part of the lithosphere, the hydrosphere and part of the atmosphere. The jump in complexity of organisation with the arrival of the first truly living, self-duplicating organisms, was immense, and thoroughly justifies the coining of a new term, even though the biosphere makes use of nothing (except increased complexity) that was not already present in the inorganic world. The old debate between 'mechanists' and 'vitalists' is seen at once to have been wholly misconceived.

It is important to grasp that at every stage in the world's history the forces of both radial and tangential energy are operative, and that although they work in some senses in opposite directions, yet they are in fact complementary. Radial energy 'borrows',

[24] Eduard Suess, *The Face of the Earth* (1909).

for instance, the heat (and other forms of thermodynamic energy) liberated 'tangentially'. It should also be noted that there is no automatic straight-line evolution – none of the kind of 'ortho-genesis' that has been so correctly discarded by biologists as not consonant with the facts. It would be astonishing if 'groping' did not lead, more often than not, into byways and blind alleys, where the radial-energy-potential slowly runs down. But if we think of the process, as Teilhard always did, in terms of the whole rather than of the individual element or group, in terms that is of *cosmogenesis*, then even the blind alleys become meaningful. For complexity-consciousness to be possible, and to go on increasing, there must be variety in the environment for consciousness to operate on. Nothing is wasted, nothing is lost, and finally all will be gathered in. The way in which this vision harmonises with that of the New Testament is at times quite staggering.

Noosphere

The next 'sphere' word was the one coined by Teilhard and le Roy in the 1920's. With the advent of thinking man as the 'leading shoot' of the biosphere (leading because of the enormous leap forward in consciousness that 'thinking' necessarily implies) the evolutionary process entered on a wholly new phase. As man has colonised the earth he has formed, within the biosphere, a meshwork of conscious communication which Teilhard calls a 'mind layer' or 'noosphere'. Man is made of the dust of the earth. But now the dust is able to reflect upon itself and, by a further extension of the 'inturning' which Teilhard makes the character-istic feature of the evolutionary process (when seen on a large enough scale), begins to know and understand what the whole business is about. That this Teilhardian way of looking at the world is beginning to be shared (though not necessarily through contact with Teilhard) by other scientists, is shown by a passage from the introduction by Professor George Wald of Harvard to the 1958 edition[25] of that remarkable work, *The Fitness of the*

[25] Macmillan.

Environment, by the late L. J. Henderson, first published in 1913. Wald finds it necessary to apologise for his startling 'new' concept, but it is certainly a justifiable one: 'Let me talk a little frank nonsense about this, make of it what you will. It would be a poor thing to be an atom in a universe without physicists. And physicists are made of atoms. A physicist is the atom's way of knowing about atoms.'

For Teilhard the noosphere is the world's way of knowing about the world. The impetus to research, exploration, investigation, becomes irresistible. But for Teilhard there is yet another step. 'Research is adoration', as was said in an earlier chapter. The evolutionary process is fundamentally religious in nature, because it manifests not only increasing consciousness but also increasing personalisation. This 'spiritual face' of the world would never have shown itself, could never have developed, if it had not been for the indwelling spirit, operative throughout time both as alpha, the source, and omega, the end.

Granted the development of the noosphere, could man have achieved what Teilhard calls 'Point Omega' by the exercise of his mind alone? As we have said, at every stage of the process, the tangential is operative, leading to dispersion at the same, or a falling, level of radial energy. Complexity-consciousness involves, as a corollary, increasing freedom from environmental constraints, increasing freedom for the organism to choose or determine its own course of action. This freedom reaches a critical level with the development of the noosphere. The temptation not to search for (or even grope for) the entrance to the next 'sphere' in the *enroulement* or 'inturning process', not to seek the spirit of love and understanding (which has been both *vis a tergo* and *vis a fronte*), the temptation to rebel is tremendous. Natural man is a natural rebel. In this setting of *anthropogenesis*, the myths of the biblical *Genesis* take on new force and new meaning.

The incarnation represents the means by which God's evolutionary purpose will be achieved, despite the natural tendency of man to use and abuse his freedom in rejecting the call to what the noosphere itself cannot offer but only hint at, namely union with

God and all his creation. Without Christ this redemption from 'sin' (what Teilhard called 'diminishments') could not have occurred. But the goal is not achieved at once. The struggle is continuous, and though individual men and women may win through to sanctity, the process will not be complete until the pleroma. This is what evolution has been for. This is what makes sense of both science and religion.

So once again, but now in terms of Christianity, Teilhard speaks of movement, dynamism, growth. With the noosphere in full spate, itself developed within the biosphere, we are now in the early stages of the Christosphere. Christ was born, suffered and died for us. There is to be the second coming. Meanwhile the Christosphere is in process of developing. Teilhard calls the process Christogenesis. The concept shows his deep appreciation of the doctrine of the mystical body of Christ, which all mankind are called to form. The ecumenical movement is deeply Teilhardian in character.

A system of thought which is as far-ranging as this clearly carries limitless implications, and has unlimited application. It will be appreciated that for Teilhard there is no question, in the Christosphere, of denying, or denigrating, or escaping from the noosphere, any more than the latter can dispense with the biosphere, nor the biosphere with atmosphere, hydrosphere or lithosphere. The whole is a seamless garment, the garment that Christ put on himself. Teilhard puts it simply, 'To think we must eat.' He goes on, 'But what a variety of thoughts we get out of one slice of bread!' To a scientist thinking in terms only of tangential energy, the thermodynamic content of a slice of bread is exactly calculable, and remains constant whether the material is fed into a combustion stove or a horse, an overfed laggard, or a hungry creative artist who will use the strength it gives him to 'produce' radial energy. In Teilhardian thinking we see the final overthrow of that apparently indestructible (as it has been called) manicheean philosophy. Before the pleroma it is necessary that every 'sphere' of created matter shall have been fully exploited; not only exploited but now, with the advent of man, fully re-created through

scientific exploration. The strength of the appeal to research into and understand each aspect of the created universe is far greater than any utilitarian philosophy can give. All such work is orientated, whether or not the fact is recognised, toward omega point. 'Everything that rises must converge.'

Teilhard's own range of interests and professional competence included some aspects of each 'layer', from inorganic to spiritual and mystic. It is important, in reading him, to be sure one is on the same 'wavelength', and to remember that a discussion, say, of some point about the noosphere will be conducted in terms appropriate to that level of organisation or complexity-consciousness. Such a respect for method makes possible the vital debate between Christian and Agnostic. Most important, a dialogue becomes possible between Christian and Marxist, to their mutual benefit. But it must always be borne in mind that within and yet beyond the noosphere lies, for Teilhard, Christogenesis, which is its goal and fulfilment, and which makes all things meaningful.

Fruits of the Teilhardian Method

In a brief exposition such as this one can do no more than indicate a few of the immensely fertile fields of inquiry that are restored or opened up by the Teilhardian method. It goes without saying that all research directed toward the discovery of how the material universe comes into existence, and of how it changes with time, is fundamental to the system. So too is research into the mechanisms of biological evolution, mechanisms that stretch into the world of pre-living macromolecules, and also into the complexities of the organisation of central nervous systems and computing machines.

But if much of this is research into the past, the pressing problem for reflective man is research into the possibilities open to the future. Psychological and sociological research is vital if man is to avoid such abuse of his new level of freedom that he destroys himself, at the very time when it is possible dimly to discern the goal that lies ahead. Mankind is necessarily 'turned in' on itself,

and must either learn to live with itself or perish. Teilhard
certainly envisages the possibility of a final death-struggle bringing ruin to the world, but he dismisses the possibility, not because
of his faith in the noogenesis to which humanism is restricted
(though this has a vast amount to contribute), but because of his
faith in Christogenesis. The birth, death and resurrection of
Christ, who came into the world in order to redeem it (including
man) cannot have been in vain.

The sociological and political applications of Teilhardian
thought are very far-reaching. The struggles of races, nations,
power-blocs, will one day come to an end as surely as did those
of individual clans and city-states. The possibility of local out-
breaks of aggression will always remain, but by and large the
world as a whole will become as peaceful as the once-warring
counties of England have become. As with counties, so with
races and countries: local loyalties will be preserved and should
be encouraged, but they will find expression in friendly rivalries
and not in anger and hatred. The fundamental oneness of the
family of man, as shown by the story of his evolution, is a fact
of the greatest importance. This is a fact about mankind which
is splendidly complemented by the thousands of minor variations
on which man's further evolution depends. The era of pure indi-
vidualism is over, and henceforth individual talents will be developed for the benefit of the community. It is in free and loving
service to his fellow-men that the individual finds himself, finds
the world and finds God.

Teilhard wrote many essays on sociological themes, essays
which introduce his daring concepts of the 'ultra-personal' and
the 'collective super-consciousness'. He seems at times to be
verging on the totalitarian 'solutions' of which this century has
seen too much already. But, while he recognises the legitimacy of
some of the strivings of totalitarian systems to date, he points
with unerring accuracy at the weakness of systems that ignore
the personal, which he sees as the central dynamic core of the
universe, the alpha-omega that is God.

Teilhard poses more questions than he solves for philosophy

and theology. His insights are profound, at times very reminiscent of St. Paul, for whose letters he had a special affection and regard. He would not claim, any more than Paul, to be an academic philosopher or theologian. But his works merit, and are currently receiving, detailed attention from the scholars. Many important commentaries have already appeared on the continent of Europe, and we can expect many more to be published, both abroad and in this country. He is essentially a seminal force of astonishing liberality and generosity (like nature itself). He outlined securely enough the broad framework of his ideas. Some of his seeds he tended carefully until they grew and flowered and came to fruiting. Many others are no more than seedlings as yet, and will need time and care before it is known whether or not they can grow. However confident he is that in broad outlines his ideas are valid and will in time be accepted by all, yet at the end of his major work of synthesis he recognises, with a characteristically true modesty,[26] that

In this arrangement of values I may have gone astray at many points. It is up to others to try to do better. My one hope is that I have made the reader feel both the reality, difficulty, and urgency of the problem and, at the same time, the scale and the form which the solution cannot escape.

[26] *The Phenomenon of Man,* p. 290.

3

Significance

A MAN whose range of thought embraces such an immensely wide field, and whose position was so thoroughly 'catholic' in the best sense of the word, is inevitably a target for criticism from many different sides. Criticism is even more certain if the writer concerned is an original and creative thinker, a pioneer who needs at times to invent a new language in order to express his insights. Professionals in the established disciplines are bound to be wary of him, and may attempt to disown him. When scientists, philosophers and theologians are only too ready to dismiss and denigrate the activities of each other as either superficial fact-grubbing, or meaningless, metaphysical nonsense, or pure mythology, anyone who has the temerity to stand square in the centre and attempt to interpret, with sympathy and understanding, the insights of each group to the others, is bound to get caught in crossfire. Teilhard is no exception. Despite the growing appreciation of the importance of his message for the future of man (social, cultural, religious) there have been and will be voices raised in protest.

Some of the protests are unquestionably justified. As pointed out earlier, some of the now published writings are no more than 'trial runs', in which ideas are tried out tentatively, and possible implications drawn. The method chosen for posthumous publication has been one more suited to an already established author, whose major achievements have been clearly delineated. Against such a background minor works of little significance can be put into focus. It is right that everything authentic should be published. One is impatient for the final volumes in the Collected Works. But the question of critical editing is important, and unfortunately Teilhardian enthusiasts have hitherto (and understandably), been too enthusiastic to be properly critical. This can lead to excessive and undeserved attack on the author himself.

The most vehement criticism of Teilhard's writing to date has come, not from the ranks of orthodox theology, but from the sometimes equally bigoted ranks of orthodox science. Sir Peter Medawar's scathing attack[27] on *The Phenomenon of Man* and its author was an excessively emotional protest against what Teilhard specifically denied at the end of the book, where he says (p. 292) 'I might be suspected of wanting to introduce an apologia by artifice.' Medawar claimed that Teilhard 'can be excused of dishonesty only on the grounds that before deceiving others he has taken great pains to deceive himself'. One would ignore his rather cheap jibe if it were not for the fact that Medawar's position as Director of a National Research Institute, combined with his popular appeal as a radio and television personality, gave his article an influence in this country altogether out of proportion to its real worth. For a reply to the criticism itself, and an attempt to interpret the underlying psychology, the reader is referred to the present writer's article, 'Scientific Master versus Pioneer.'[28] Medawar's attack will have only temporarily held up the serious study of Teilhard's phenomenology by the scientifically trained, and there are signs that the setback is already in part overcome. On the Continent the importance of Teilhard as a thinker is well recognised by major scientists, who do not necessarily accept all his hypotheses, nor even, as yet, the validity of all the evidence he adduced in their support.

We might expect scientists of the positivist–humanist school of philosophy to object to the conclusions Teilhard draws from his examination of the phenomena. In postulating a God who is the 'ground of our being' he will no more gain the support of agnostics than will any other man who uses such theological language. But Teilhard has the advantage over some contemporary theologians in that an unprejudiced scientist (and most scientists *are* relatively unprejudiced) will recognise his

[27] *Mind*, Vol. 70 (1961), No. 277, pp. 99–106.
[28] *The Listener*, 15 April, 1965.

methodology as sound. That is all that Teilhard asks, because thereafter the facts of nature can be allowed to speak for themselves.

Philosophical and theological objections to Teilhard came during his lifetime not only from some of his superiors in the Jesuit Order, but also from the theologians of the Holy Office, and in particular the distinguished Dominican Père Garrigou-Lagrange O.P. Since his death other Dominicans have published critical studies, particularly Olivier Rabut O.P. in France,[29] and Cornelius Ernst O.P.[30] in this country.

It is interesting that these members of the Order to which St. Thomas Aquinas belongs should be specially critical of one who may well come to be regarded as the Aquinas of the twentieth century. Teilhard's dynamic and open system ought to be capable of protecting itself from the fate that overtook the majestic synthesis of Aquinas, that of being strait-jacketed into a system of propositions confined to the manuals of dogmatic theology. Within the Dominican Order itself, of course, Thomistic thought is lively and flexible. In time, perhaps, it will show itself to be flexible enough to accommodate a natural successor to 'the angelic doctor'.

Of the critics mentioned the most sympathetic is Rabut, who opens his final chapter with the following,

> Those who condemn Teilhard should try to go one better; they should start by sharing with him, and in the same degree, his secret perceptions of contemporary thought – thought which is new and living. Whatever his shortcomings, Teilhard attains a kind of objectivity, a peculiar rightness, through certain outstanding qualities which we should try to learn from him.

The theological problem is to see how far it is possible to re-interpret, in the light of modern knowledge about cosmogenesis, not only the gospels, but all developed Christian doctrine, that

[29] *Dialogue avec Teilhard de Chardin*, 1959 (translated 1961).
[30] *The Clergy Review*, Vol. 46 (1961), pp. 223–234.

has been formulated for nineteen centuries in language appropriate to the common-sense view that the world is fundamentally static in organisation or cyclical in its operations. Teilhard de Chardin has shown at least how the rethinking can be done. In doing so he has run the risk of being labelled 'heretic' on any one of half a dozen charges. The pantheism which appears to underlie some of his mystical appreciations of the 'spirit of the earth' is both fully understood, and categorically denied by him, in one of the most important essays he ever wrote ('Mon Univers', included in *Écrits du Temps de la Guerre*). He has been said to deny the possibility of individual immortality, and yet we have seen earlier how he regarded death. He has been charged with neglect of the problem of evil, and especially of 'original sin'.

Some of his writings on these topics are not yet published, and any judgment is premature. But the treatment of evil and suffering (in terms of 'diminishments') in *Le Milieu divin*, and his 1933 essay entitled 'The meaning and constructive value of suffering,'[31] have found a response among Christians and non-Christians alike. One begins really to see, to understand and accept what has hitherto made sense only in terms of a retributive 'justice' that creates great difficulties in understanding the goodness of God. It has been objected that St. Paul's pleroma is a supernatural concept which Teilhard degrades by linking it too closely with the natural world. But this traditional interpretation of the pleroma was the result of a neo-Platonic dualism which the Christian world must be prepared to abandon if it is to survive. When the world has completed its 'groaning and travailling', and brought the pleroma to birth, Teilhard looks forward with Paul to the time when 'God shall be all in all'. This highly mysterious utterance is now seen, taken literally, to make very good sense. It provides a goal which is supremely worth working toward.

It is well not to judge Teilhard on the basis of only one or two of his books. In some ways it is a pity that it was his most difficult (because most fully integrating) work, *The Phenomenon of Man*,

[31] Published in N. Braybrooke (ed.), *Teilhard de Chardin: Pilgrim of the Future.* Also in *The Sunday Times*, 11 April, 1965.

that first brought his name to the attention of the public. His shorter essays, dealing with particular aspects of his system, show his true *métier*, and some of them are hardly known as yet. A valuable and detailed guide-book to most of his writings is that by Emile Rideau S.J. entitled *La Pensee du Père Teilhard de Chardin* (Editions du Seuil, 1965). Some of his critics have undoubtedly been too hasty and rash in their condemnations, just as some of his supporters have been rash in their enthusiasms. Violent reactions are the legacy and hallmark of genuine pioneers. So rapid and efficient is the modern network of communications that we might expect the emotional storm to subside more rapidly than some. The real work will then begin, of consciously 'building the earth' in Teilhardian terms.

Teilhard is no naïve optimist, as he has been portrayed, preaching only sweetness and hope. He knew what it is to suffer, and he saw beyond the pain. He speaks directly to a technological age in turmoil, an age where despair is never far away from the sophisticated living that science has made possible. Eight hundred years ago Aquinas tackled the pagan world of classical science and philosophy, and brought its intellectual benefits within the Christian fold. Teilhard, with a vastly more complex situation to deal with, has done the same by a method wholly appropriate to the situation. His name will one day be linked with that of Aquinas. And then, with Dominican and Jesuit so joined, love and understanding will be found where they should always begin, at home, in the church. These two great Christian humanists proclaim again, to a world in need, that 'God so loved *the world* that he sent his only-begotten son'.

PRINCIPAL WORKS BY TEILHARD DE CHARDIN, AVAILABLE IN ENGLISH

The Divine Milieu, 1960
The Future of Man, 1964
Hymn of the Universe, 1965
Letters from a Traveller, 1962
The Making of a Mind: Letters from a Soldier-Priest 1914-1919, 1965
The Phenomenon of Man, 1959

All published by Harper

Commentaries in English:

Teilhard de Chardin: A Biographical Study, by Claude Cuénot. Taplinger, 1965

Memories of Teilhard de Chardin, by Helmut de Terra. Harper, 1965

Teilhard de Chardin: Scientist and Seer, by C. E. Raven. Harper, 1963

In the Field with Teilhard de Chardin, by George B. Barbour. Herder and Herder, 1965

Teilhard de Chardin: Pilgrim of the Future, edited by Neville Braybrooke. Seabury, 1964

Pierre Teilhard de Chardin: His Life and Spirit, by N. Corte. Translation and preface by M. Jarrett-Kerr. Macmillan, 1960

Dialogue with Teilhard de Chardin, by O. A. Rabut. Sheed and Ward, 1961

Teilhard de Chardin and the Mystery of Christ, by Christopher F. Mooney. Harper, 1966

DATE DUE

DEMCO 38-297